LOVE SONGS

FOR A COUNTRY LANE

Grant King

ISBN 13: 978-1883197490
ISBN 10: 188319749X

10 9 8 7 6 5 4 3 2 1

CONTENTS

Foreword – Chris Gantry
Preface – David Peel

II.   On a Country Road (Poems)

About the Author

FOREWORD

How to be so wise and yet so young ." It was this perception of Grant King that astounded me every time I was around him, which was a lot starting in 1964. We were still boy/men striking out in Nashville, Tennessee as aspiring songwriters. It was the time of cultural revolution in the country-- fertile soil for art and however far one wanted to take it. There was a clique of young writers that hung out together, each one gleaning a new perspective in the outburst of creativity taking place across America. Grant King was one of them, inquisitive, thought-provoking with his persistent razor sharp comments on life, love, art, and the human condition. I was a loner, myself, but I gravitated to Grant because I was aware that he was exceptional in his pursuits. I loved listening to his commentaries about song-writing and poetry, they were astute, deep, and helped to energize my own dreams. Grant was a thoughtful dreamer, a ponderer, like the statue of THE THINKER. Now here he is a zillion light years later, still the dreamer with a love for the process that's never left him, an elder statesman of the world with a collection of his poetry. Poetry that spans the life of the man. Poetry concretized and wrapped up into this lovely eclectic collection. Poetry that only Grant could write. I was blessed to be around him when I was, I learned a lot from him.

-Chris Gantry

Singer, Songwriter, Nashville Recording Artist

PREFACE

A couple of months back, I was rummaging through some old publicity photos, press releases, etc; all reflecting a music career that has now spanned some 50 years. There among these treasures, I found something that I think I'll cherish forever. As a matter of fact, it will soon be framed and placed on my office wall. It's simply a weekly record playlist from country radio station WMTS in Murfreesboro, Tennessee. That particular week, the program director (Ron Nelson) had charted my new single release, "Wax Museum," NUMBER ONE! The writer was none other than Grant King, one of Nashville's finest new writers. You just can't imagine the excitement I felt back then to have a number 1 hit in Murfreesboro, a small town just a few miles from where I was raised. That year, I was a bona-fide star among relatives and friends I grew up with in the area. I had finally come "home" to country music; having been a drifting folk singer in coffee houses on the west coast since college. I had recently signed with Nashville's first
independent record label, Chart Records. My first release on Chart was actually a remake of the Fats Domino classic, "I'm Walkin'." To everyone's amazement, it was quickly heard on radio stations everywhere. DJs loved the record's upbeat instrumentals from some of Music City's finest, accompanying musicians. It wasn't until "Wax Museum," however, with its haunting melody and poignant lyrics that country radio began to seriously take notice of myself as an artist. I enjoy performing it even to this day.
Thank you Grant for this incredible song and for the role "Wax Museum"
played in kick-starting my career. Your collection of songs and poetry here is a treasure and a lasting tribute to you as a gifted writer.
"Welcome to the Wax Museum,
Visit with the folks who live within the walls..."

-David Peel
DavidPeelMusic.com

LUSTIN' FOR LOVE

Songs

"Were you lovin' for lust or just lustin' for love."

-Grant King

Anna's Diner

Anna's Diner sat top of Monteagle
I'd always stop in on a run
Best food in the world that was legal
Best eatin' t'was under the sun

That mountain was rough on us truckers
There was always somebody that died
You'd hear all the stories and details
As soon as you stepped up inside

We knew 41 was a killer
The chances of dying were real
We were glad of the interstate's coming
Never knew if we were eatin' our last meal

The smell was of green beans and collards
Mash taters and gravy and chops
The coffee and tea with a plain meat and three
Was such it would make your tongue flop

But then the interstate took it
The parking lot "right-of-wayed" through
Old Anna's kept trying to struggle
'Til they finally fenced it off, too.

Now Anna's just lives in old drivers
As stories begin to commence
Of the best trucker's meal there was ever
For three dollars and forty-five cents

09/30/2013

Bad Words

Bad words - I got bad words inside of me
Bad words - They got no place to hide in me
Bad words - keep coming out in spite of me
Ugliest kind of stuff you ever heard - bad words

Does this dress make me fat ? No, you already are
She's had enough, can't take this stuff and drives off in the car
Two weeks she'll be back again - she's stayin' with her sister
And when she does come through the door she'll ask me if I missed her

Chorus

I stumble to the kitchen, gotta think to use my legs
She's all bright and perky "Do you want me to make eggs ?"
No, just cook the ones we bought there in the refrigerator
Then once more she's out the door - she'll be back two weeks later

Chorus

She says I never hug her - Well, my arms won't reach around
Thirty minutes later and I wake up on the ground
She says I have no filter - that I'm only trying to guilt her
And says she's gonna quit on me - "Well, as long as you don't sit on me "

Chorus

Bored

I'm bored - I admit it
There's no more fun in store - I get it
The stuff that used to be a bash
Now usually costs me too much cash
There's no more good time livin' to look forward
I'm bored

It's dull ya know
My excitement cup feels empty when it's full
And though
Like molding squash in the refrigerator
A girl my age is too old to date her
And if I did - no joy to be encored
I'm bored

It's hard to be so charming
When the dust bunny farm I'm farming
Has more wrangling bunnies than I thought could be ignored
We all know I can do it
I'm totally up to it
My naps will help me through it mightily snored
I'm bored

Cheap Motel Soap

She came home smelling of cheap motel soap
There wasn't too much I could say
I knew the smell from my travelling
She had travelled too far in one day

So I complimented her new perfume
And told her it smelled so sweet
That I'd smelled it before as I shopped store to store
Lots of ladies were wearing it ... on the street

I could have done something ugly
Her cheating drove me to the brink
But I left her in peace in her own sin and grease
And left ten motel soaps on her sink

She can't wash away all that cheating
Or the lies and despair and lost hope
It's more than just rinse and repeating
It takes more than just cheap motel soap

Country Miss

Writin' tunes and passin' time
It's just like treadin' water
Current flows me down the line
As days keep gettin' shorter

Got my guitar, fiddle too
A note pad I can write on
Work a song up 'til it's through
One I can play all night on

Bridge: Miss, miss, gimme little kiss
      Welcome to my tune emporium
      I'm the reason that they call it
      The Rhymin' Auditorium

Won't make the Billboard Top 100
Won't try to get it cut
Those vampires never suck these veins
I'm not that kinda nut

Forty years of Music City
Had my run of Nashville
Took their BS smilin' pretty
But not because I'm bashville

Not tryin' to write no country hit
I'm best at writin' misses
This tune has that perfect fit
That's exactly just what this is

Bridge: Miss, miss, gimme little kiss
      Welcome to my tune emporium
      I'm the reason that they call it
      The Rhymin' Auditorium

10/30/2013

Crimson and Blue

At the end of the day when the light slips away
And the skies turn to crimson and blue
With the day safe behind me the evenings find me
Alone as they usually do

And it won't hurt a thing if the phone never rings
I'll remember old times with a tune
Of the softest red hair and blue eyes - it's unfair
As the evening passes so soon

It's a pretty good bet I may never forget
I try not to fret - yet, I do
I can't put her behind me when skies still remind me
How much I'm enjoying the view
Remembering her crimson and blue

September 2006

Floor

Chorus: Floor, oh floor, my dearest friend
    I'm back to visit once again
    You're my bestest friend of all
    You always catch me when I fall

Her heart rejects me, threw me out
I'll never know what that's about
Just drag me home and shut the door
I'll lay with my old friend once more

The wine it tricks me, let it pour
And for a time my thoughts will soar
Then slowly as the room will spin
I'm down here with you once again

Chorus

There'll come a day perhaps not long
When all my rights meet all my wrongs
When spirit leaves, my soul will climb
I'll lay with you one final time

Should Heaven's gate assess my sins
I'll beg, I'll plead "Please let me in"
I know there's room for just one more
Who'll gladly sleep on Heaven's floor

Chorus

Grace

Safe in God's sweet Holy Grace
I'll cling unto my Savior's Cross
And in His promise and embrace
I'll safely sail my oceans tossed

Chorus: Sweet Grace   God's Grace
              Binding me making me whole
              Your Grace   Pure Grace
              Thank you for saving my soul

Shine me down Thy Light above
And save me from this world of dare
Warm me with Eternal Love
And hear me in my softest prayer

Chorus

So lift me up and heal my heart
With Jesus' Blood's eternal flame
Though evil vents to cleave apart
I'll always cling to Jesus' Name

Chorus

Though ill winds blow and test my grasp
I'll hold His Cross until that day
That with my final breath I gasp
"In Jesus Holy Name I pray"

Chorus x2

Carol Manston/Grant King
11/08/2013

Harley

I got aspirin for my knees and my shoulder
I got Tums when my stomach goes sour
But no prescription for her heart growing colder
No doctor to call this late hour

It starts five AM with the rooster
And builds like a saddle on a burr
No shot I can take and no booster
To rid me of thinking of her

All the memories of eatin' good cookin'
And the nights of hot bunny lovin'
I'll miss more than all her good lookin'
And the smell of hot biscuits in her oven

It wasn't my gambling and boozing
I don't think I worked her too hard
Fact is I knew I was losin'
When she saw my new Harley in the yard

I don't want to sound like a whiner
With so little I've left of my pride
But if I want a pretty girl at the diner
I climb on my Harley and ride

How Much More

How much more can a poor man take
I'm battered and bruised like I stepped on a rake
Ain't got no more heart to break
Tell me how much more can a poor man take

Went to the house and the locks were changed
All the furniture rearranged
Poor little woman must be deranged
She locked me out like a dog with the mange

I went to the bank but the money was gone
The manager says I should move along
What'd I do to get treated this wrong
She better watch out - she'll sing a new song

Went to the preacher to find out why
Prayed to Jesus 'cause I'm not shy
Went to the bottle 'til the bottle went dry
I'm all outta tears got no more to cry

How much more can a poor man take
I'm battered and bruised like I stepped on a rake
Ain't got no more heart to break
Tell me how much more can a poor man take

Ill Winds

The ill winds blow down from the higher Sierra
And crinkle the leaves on the branches
But the wind that is worse does blow with a curse
From the pants of Renaldo del Sanchez

It's the dead greasy meat saved with spices so sweet
That he cooks for his own poor famille
With spices so hot that they burn through the pot
Of his daily diet of tortillas

We're all related to Sanchez
A fact that everyone knows
We succumb to ill wind avalanches
When they cover us from our heads to our toes

And when winds don't blow east and they smell like dead beast
'Cross the southern border Texas ranches
The cowboys all know it's the ill winds that blow
From the pants of Renaldo del Sanchez

It's Raining

It's raining today in the Great Smoky Mountains
The colored fall leaves are soon gone
One more good breeze and they'll all drop with ease
God's cycle of life marches on

I'll grab a new log for the fire place
And a hot cup of coffee for me
The crackle and sizzle with rain's steady drizzle
And the view out the window is free

I'll sit on the couch with a blanket
There's time for a good mountain tune
I'll grab up my fiddle and play just a little
And smile when the cat leaves the room

It's raining today in the Great Smoky Mountains
Inside I will have no regrets
The gentle refrain from the soft mountain rain
Makes this life as good as it gets

Kissing Mad

I love kissing your temper
I love to kiss when you're mad
It's more fun than just with a whimper
The best kisses I've ever had

Your worst kiss is screaming delicious
Typical of girls here down south
I'm not talking malicious
But you've got a pretty big mouth

Whenever you're quiet it's alarming
I know that I give you hard times
Kissing you soft is disarming
And it feels more to me like a crime

So tease you I will 'til you're fuming
I'll prod 'til you're madder than hell
When that voice from your mouth comes a'booming
It's easier to find when you yell

5/ 28/1995

Let the Children Be Children

The children were loud, their excitement grew
Wondering what was this crowd gathered out of the blue
Their parents had brought them for Jesus to bless
But disciples were holding them back from the rest

'Til they made such commotion it caught Jesus' ear
And He called for the children, He gathered them near
The Son of all sons who would teach them to pray
Spoke up for the children and all heard Him say

"Let the children be children
Suffer them come unto Me
Let the children be children
For of such is what Heaven shall be"

He spoke to them gently and tender
These children who'd often heard worse
At last they had found their Defender
At last someone placing them first

And He laid hands upon them and blessed them
As His spirit would have Him to do
So when later life's challenges test them
They'd always have One to turn to

"Let the children be children
Suffer them come unto Me
Let the children be children
For of such is what Heaven shall be"

05/28/1998

Lustin' For Love

I was chancin' romancin' right after a break
Too soon to go mooney that was a mistake
Snuck up on my blind side three-sixty degrees
With my heart in my hands and down on my knees

Bridge: Were you lovin' for lust or lustin' for love
Were you dealin' with feelin's you know nothing of
Were you riskin' your friskin' to stars up above
Were you lovin' for lust or just lustin' for love

I was rushin' and crushin' your blushin' too soon
All your kissin' I'm missin' was bliss in the moon
We never stopped laughin' and gettin' along
Then six months to the day and then *phlllllttt* you were gone

Now I'm humblin' and stumblin' and crumblin' again
Gettin' used to abuse and then loosin' the hand
Should I chase you and face you and place you in cuffs
Or rein in the painin' and holler "Enough"

Bridge: Were you lovin' for lust or just lustin' for love
Were you dealin' with feelin's you know nothing of
Were you riskin' your friskin' to stars up above
Were you lovin' for lust or just lustin' for love

Were you lovin' for lust or just lustin' for love

10/23/2013

Mountains of North Carolina

Nothing but stars out my window
Nothing but trout in my creeks
December through June the fog lifts by noon
Brushing tears of God's joy on His peaks

I'm through with the asphaulted cities
Concrete canyons that go on for miles
And the same row of houses with duplicate spouses
Bragging on their 1.3 childs

Just give me the high mountain meadows
Deep hollows enfolded between
And clouds as they pass through the tall flowered grass
It's the prettiest view that I've seen

When time comes to meet with Saint Peter
I'll make that transition just fine
As long as heaven's as green as half what I've seen
In these mountains of North Caroline
    Smoky Mountains of North Caroline

September 2006

Musical Brew

It starts with a fire in the belly
It takes that to boil down the corn
Add a little twang from a Tele
That's how a good song gets born

Write about Romeo and Juliette
Curse Adolph and cold Eva Braun
But deep down inside we're all Bonnie and Clyde
We're a mixture of what's right and what's wrong

Chorus: Drink me - let the Dixie Cups drown
        Drink me - swallow every word down
        I'll keep paintin' my passion on pages - rewarded with air guitar wages
        Sellin' my brew like the smart 'shiners do - giving free drinks all around

Beware the long arm of justice
Cold hearts that critique from afar
All that sugar and yeast make a powerful beast
And they don't approve love from a jar

Distill the spirit to essence
Condense it all back to a steam
The words as they cool make repressible fools
To believe in impossible dreams

Chorus

New Year's Eve

My New Year's Resolution is to not make one at all
A silly game I play the same each year
As soon as it gets spoken - the resolution's broken
Just idle sound with no one 'round to hear

This year's celebration may turn out to be short
You took care of that in court I do believe
I'll celebrate but then I'll probably be in bed by ten
No joys in makin' noise this New Year's Eve

Chorus: But I promise I won't smoke - I promise I won't drink
         And I won't cuss and think of us I swear
         While I light my cigarette and sip my margarita
         I'll be damned if I'll admit that I still care

It's said two people marry with a promise that they carry
A promise made in Heaven - not on Earth
When the promise doesn't fit - they give up and they quit
So tell me someone what's a promise worth ?

Chorus: I'll be damned if I'll admit - maybe someday I may quit
         But I'll be damned if I'll admit that I still care

6/20/1991

Old Bridge Road

There's a graveyard down off Old Bridge Road
On a mound back under the trees
Safe from the Okefenokee
And the gators and cypress knees

No one knows who's buried there
Bare stones tell no tales
No families ever lived back there
There's no roads, no paths, no trails

I've been there in the daytime
And it still didn't feel too right
Nothing but moss and crawfish holes
I'm sure not going back at night

It's not too far from that old bridge
Where the waters run cool and deep
And when the wind blows up from down behind
You'd swear you could hear them weep

I still fish the old bridge after dark
And I probably always will
But when you feel feet on the boards behind
That's when you sit real still

Old Guitar

There's an old guitar leaned in the corner
It's covered with a layer of dust
The tuners are stickin' - it needs a good pickin'
The strings are starting to rust

I used to pick it more often
To make up a new song to play
But with age my passion has softened
And I just don't have that much to say

Chorus: I remember the good times in Nashville
      People waved on Music Row and they smiled
      With songs in the charts I broke all the girls' hearts
      I was cock of the walk for a while

Chords fight each other in the moonlight
Like dead strings on a pawn shop guitar
The notes die faster than a sermon from the pastor
Monday mornin' when they open the bar

Now I write just for me and the giggles
It usually comes on without warning
If I drink just enough I can write some great stuff
But it doesn't make sense in the morning

Chorus: I remember the good times in Nashville
      People waved on Music Row and they smiled
      I'm still searching for answers for those damned bronze nude dancers
      The city council dropped on 16th like a pile

So the old guitar leans in the corner
There's a reason I treat it so poor
I don't want to sing what the old memories bring
I just don't want to hurt anymore

No I don't want to write all this sad crap tonight
I just don't want to hurt anymore

Old Pain

I wish this time when she broke it
It had broken more like a bone
That evil goodbye as she spoke it
Won't let it heal up on its own

It's muscle and blood and sinew
It's torn and hemorrhaging deep
When spasms rack constantly in you
It's almost impossible to sleep

Chorus

It starts with a throb when I'm waking
Pain increases throughout the day
In the evening my hands will stop shaking
As I put the last bottle away

Yes I drink to that inevitable curing
With time both a curse and a friend
To the pain of a love this enduring
And the sleep I'll enjoy in the end

Chorus: Old pain, sweet pain, a dubious friend
      My constant companion, you're always around
      Old pain, sweet pain, right to the end
      She'll never let go 'til I'm dead in the ground

Old Stains

I get home from work and her feelin's still there
So I'm cleaning the house just to freshen the air
The cleaners I'm usin' replace her perfume
But her memory lingers in every room

I washed all the curtains, I've dusted the place
'Hid all her pictures and still see her face
Read all the fine print on bottles I've used
But none of it tells how to clean out the blues

Chorus: I tried Ajax and Lysol and black Jack and beer
Her stain won't wash out while her memory's still here
But I found a cleaner that cleans this heart bright
I'm cleaning old stains out with Paula tonight

She's fast, she's efficient, leaves no tell-tale ring
Soothing to the eyes and smells sweet as spring
Hard working, long lasting and makes this boy shine
If I've learned my lesson I'll treat this one fine

Chorus

Re-gifting

I'm re-gifting a re-gifted gift
It was given by someone - a true giving thrifter
Since it's better to give than receive as we live
I'm a re-gifting re-gifted re-gifter

I've re-gifted it two or three times
Each time it returns to the scene of the crimes
I could save the new giver the cost to deliver
I'd be saving them nickels and dimes

So get ready it's your turn to get it
It's the lamest of gifts and you'll never forget it
Just remember who gave it and if you don't save it
If it comes back to me you'll regret it

10/26/2013

Rita Blue

Found a job in another state
Had to move - it wouldn't wait
We held each other and said goodbye
Only time I saw her cry

Arms entwined we promised then
To keep in touch now and again
The lasting memory brought to view
Is gazing into Rita's blue

Bridge: Rita Blue   Rita Blue
        Tortured soul what did I do
        Lost the only love for me
        Left Rita Blue in Tennessee

To this day we sometimes write
I think about her every night
And watch the dark when stars shine through
And don't have to gaze into Rita's blue

My heart still pumps though slow and deep
And forces me my thoughts to keep
With flowing love in humble pain
Pumps Rita blue through every vein

Bridge

Roadkill

That shiny slick spot that you see on life's roadway
It's not just another roadkill
It's the very same spot you ran over my heart
And you're doin' it just for the thrill....
Love's splattered all over your grill

I thought I saw stars but it was your headlights
Your love flattened me just like a truck
You made such an impact I know I'm a sight
Now isn't this my kind of luck....
I'm not only flattened I'm stuck

I don't feel so lonely - your slick spots abound
You flattened all those who'd afford ya
It's not like we're tracking a deer on hard ground
More like following Sherman through Georgia

So as you go driving down life's lonely highway
Remember those spots on the road
Have mercy on me and steer clear if you see
That's not just some other toad....
That's me and my heart on the road
Me and my heart on the road....

June 1995

Rooster

Saturday's gone - mule's in the shed
Workday is done and it's time for bed
Bank the fire and clean the pot
A prayer of thanks for what we got

Rooster will crow - church bell calls
Dress up in Sunday overalls
Sing old hymns with voice in tune
Then fiddle on the porch all afternoon

Evening comes so cap the jar
Monday morning's not too far
Pray the Lord for clearer skies
And a dollar for church if the rooster cries

Saxophone

I don't need no "better half"
I can have fun all alone
When the need comes for a laugh
I just play my saxophone

And play the notes about half right
Not in order but with ease
Toot that baby through the night
Honkin' like a flock of geese

Laugh so hard my sides are splittin'
Squeaky highs and basso tone
When times get tough I don't think quittin'
I just play my saxophone

All the news is too damn sad
Don't worry like they want me to
Blow them notes out good or bad
Keep wailing til they're black and blue

10/20/2013

Searching

If I could change eternity and win my future back
Would it cancel my infirmities and put me on the track
Or eliminate my gambling against the years of pain
From all the late night ramblings where truth was sought in vain

Somewhere there lies an answer between this written line
You'd think the right enhancer would be a glass of wine
But here down near the bottom where I still feel so perplexed
This glass of wine ain't got 'em so I think I'll pour the next

I've looked for answers high and low I've scouted far and wide
The problem must be in plain sight - There's no place left to hide
If no answer is forthcoming before this bottle's through
I'll pop cork on another - I love searching - yes I do

Unbroken

If you lose her go and find her
Just remember don't remind her
Leave the pain of loss unspoken
Love rewards a heart unbroken

Give her love and give her kisses
Be the everything she misses
Raise her children straight and strong
So they may miss her when she's gone

And come the day when hope deceives you
Logic fails and love will leave you
Hold good memories soft and dear
As if the past is always here

10/14/2013

Witch

It wasn't my fault you put me under your spell
You made me feel like heaven when you put me through hell
Made me see stars when you rained in my face
I was poisoned by your potion, love, leather and lace

Kudos to the voodoo that you do with your boohoo
Applause for all you cause with your paws making juju
Lovin' in your coven was nothin' short of wonder
I'm still shakin' from your bakin' up the spell you got me under

Your fog has receded and I have succeeded
I never repeated your darkening my door
I've never had a craving for your black and witchy raving
I'll never be enslaved by your magic anymore

A dash of insecurity - a cup of cloudy weather
A sprinkling of immaturity and you boil them all together
A bottle of Jack Daniels and then throw away the brew
And drink a glass of whiskey celebrating losing you

ON A COUNTRY ROAD

Poems

"I guess my feet know where they want me to go
Walking on a country road."

- -James Taylor

Animal Gardening

My carrots are eaten by rabbits
The lettuce is ruined by deer
Potato bugs chew like potato bugs do
They're so loud I swear I can hear

Blue jays are pecking the peaches
Woodpeckers pecking the pears
I'm feeding the animals who are eating like cannibals
And wonder if anyone cares

I sprinkle cayenne on the garden
But the animals are just getting fat
They knock on my door and they ask me for more
And "can I add some tabasco to that?"

Another Week

It's just a Monday plain and simple
Like a smile without a dimple
Keep it quiet - keep it meek
It's just a day to start the week

Tuesday - that's another thing
A glint of hope the week may bring
To plan ahead good times one day
The best excuse for shedding Monday

Wednesday sneaks in like a snake
No time to swerve or hit the brake
Rivers of time are flowing swollen
Another day that's swiftly stolen

Thursday is an easy ride
Another day to take in stride
No sense this late to object
Again a screwed day to reflect

Fridays used to be so fine
A couple always comes to mind
Now they sing a different tune
Like pouring salt into the wound

Saturdays are numb as hell
A feeling that I know too well
Weekends taunt me every time
They ought to be a major crime

Sunday comes without the fluff
To end my week just soon enough
A few more hours I'll make it through
Another week now without you

Away

Away from the city, away from the buzz
The crooks and the criminals, the scams and the fuzz
Away to the land of ephemeral dreams
Of mountains and hollows in emerald greens

Trade canyons of chimneys and coughing up soot
For cool mountain fog and the moss underfoot
And tales of ancestors who lived off the land
Who will impart their skills when we need them again

Then the world and its misery dissolves in the air
As we realize our dreams and thank God we're there
May the sun in its glory bring warmth to our soul
And prepare us for Heaven, one step nearer our goal

Better Now

I'm better now, I'll keep in touch
Time has healed old wounds
I'm not drinking near as much
I don't walk room to room

My pressure's back to normal
I'm off to bed by nine
Not dressing quite as formal
This old bathrobe works just fine

To lose someone turns heart to wood
And leaves me empty hands
I never had a dog that good
I doubt I will again

Blood On the Bridge

There's blood on a bridge down in Selma
From the billy-clubs swinging with hate
And the dogs and the troopers that held them
Blood protected by layers of paint

The flow of the waters beneath it
Like the passing of clouds overhead
Won't wash out the honor bequeathed it
Nor the memory of all those who bled

And lest we forget their endeavors
Binding pasts to futures for all
Paint seals those memories forever
Over blood for the peaceful who fall

Cherish the memories of fallen
And those passed on to the Lord
The next time freedom comes calling
May we all be of one accord

Breakfast

Crack an egg down in the bowl
Crack another'n fresh and cold
Special spices sprinkled in
And olive oil to magic spin

Scrambled eggs and sausage fried
Good as Heaven, gone and died
Doubled toast and buttered hot
Jellied up or maybe not

Coffee black in a bigger cup
Almost worth the waking up
It's not the time for cooking cheap
Cook it big or back to sleep

Cable Is Out

My cable is out - the TV is black
Internet's gone - may not be back

Trouble code in a little box square
If they're sending that signal the trouble is there

Cable guy says he'll send the first man in
I've heard that before - let the weekend begin

No contact with the world - a bad feeling in my gut
No TV - no internet - I'll have to get off my butt !

But wait - I can sit and write poems and pout
If I can find something worth writing about

Cars

Life is like a tennis match
You win some and you lose
Those losses you remember most
Will make you sing the blues

The ones that haunt me still the most
I thank my lucky stars
Are not of life and loves I chose
No, these are thoughts of cars

The '60 MGB I sold
The first one in the states
Serial number 255
Worth a fortune at this date

The '60 Corvette had to go
We were newlyweds with bills
I should have kept the Vette, I know
It gave me bigger thrills

But late the nightmares wake me
Heartbroken eyelids droop
In teenage pain they take me
Back to selling my '40 Ford Coupe

Choices

I thought I knew it in my soul
But now I'm not so sure
If certainty were good as gold
You'd have to call me poor

The choices I have made in life,
The list goes on and on,
Have caused me every kind of strife
Almost every choice was wrong

Schooling, jobs, career and such
Were wrong, I won't pretend
This late it doesn't matter much
I chose you as my friend

Christmas Cheer

All my friends of Christmas past
Have gone ahead and left me last
Old friends and kinfolk, good relations
Leave little joy for celebration

But this leaves one thing to do
To find more friends, relations new
To search out those who share my plight
And celebrate this Christmas night

We'll raise a glass and give a toast
To those we lost and miss the most
And challenge all with Christmas cheer
To meet again this time next year

Christmas Gift

Balsam fronds stretch to the ceiling
Smells that bring the Christmas feeling
Blinking lights that never stop
Lovely angel on the top

Favorite ornaments hanging down
Presents laying all around
Tinsel sprinkled here and there
Makes us want to stop and stare

Children bursting from their beds
Wrapping paper torn to shreds
Where's that present Heavenly priced ?
Who wrapped the gift of Jesus Christ ?

Christmas Smells

I'm warming up my ancient nose
For Christmas smells that beckon
And fonder memories that they pose
A childish wish I reckon

Of beef stew warming, candied yams
My Grandma's kitchen brewing
Collard greens and honey ham
Old cooking smells renewing

Cinnamon on pudding bowls
Apple pie with allspice wasting
Eggnog glasses count untold
And getting chased for tasting

One smell keeps the Christmas feel
For this old sneaky stepper
The spice from Grandma's every meal
Hot black McCormick pepper

Clock

There's a clock on the wall in my bedroom
It stopped at ten minutes to eight
I've replaced the batteries weekly
They all endure the same fate

I've decided to leave it there hanging
To allow it to have its own say
To be wrong at all other moments
and right just two times a day

The hands on the poor clock are useless
Pretty much like these hands of mine
Stalled out in a world that is ruthless
Overwhelmed with the passing of time

With age my day passes slowly
And almost stands still if I wait
The next minute always surprising
Living life at ten minutes to eight

Comfort Food

What's all this talk of comfort food
Sounds purdy vain to me
I get plenty comfort
Eatin' any food I see

Try growing up in poverty
Where food was scarce to none
You appreciate the least you ate
When food was more than fun

Some years when the crops were poor
We weren't reduced to beggars
If anything would grow for sure
It was damned old rutabagas

When I think of comfort
I don't rule any food out
Except for rutabagas
And my mother's sauerkraut

So fill my plate and then stand back
I'll clean it while you're lookin'
The only food that's better'n mine
Is anybody else's cookin'

Diamonds

Some folks are lovely diamonds
They sparkle and they shine
And reflect the extra effort
That it took to make them fine

The many hours of cutting
The grinding wheel that spins
Can make the sparkles glitter
And hide the flaws within

Then some of us aren't brilliant
Our outsides coarse and tough
But still just as resilient
We're diamonds in the rough

Dig

Dig a hole and dig it deep
Place your worries there to keep
Cover loosely now to store
In case you need to add some more

And place a stone to mark it well
So years to come you still may tell
That here upon this hallowed sod
You gave your troubles all to God

Dream

Now I lay me down to sleep
Though I don't doubt it won't come fast
The problems of this day run deep
Solutions scattered far and vast

Electric bills are out of sight
We're losing jobs, our debt increases
Terrorists crossing open borders
Our Constitution shred to pieces

Muslims killing Christians more
Children dying in Darfur
Iran's going to get the bomb
Our middle class has joined the poor

That's OK I'll close my eyes
And clear those thoughts that make me cringe
Just think old cars and girlfriends fair
Then snore like hell - that's my revenge

Ducks

It isn't my job keeping ducks in a row
They're all free to wander wherever they go
And they have my unconditional backing
For waddling 'round with their incessant quacking

If I should be guilty of any time squandered
It's chasing down errant ducks who have wandered
It just doesn't pay to keep looking back
And hoping to hear that prodigal quack

This late in years it's crucial to prove
One doesn't need orderly ducks to move
I'm traveling forward to never look back
Trusting I'm followed by disorganized quacks

Eagle's Wind

Slow it down and spread it wide
So like a sky-bound river friend
Soaring soft at Heaven's side
A lofted eagle plies the wind

Knowing neither why nor how
To trust his wings and catch it there
So high above the here and now
He rules his kingdom from the air

A swoop, a turn to find the breeze
Feathers feeling every gust
What looks like floating 'round with ease
He finds the wind--he flies, he must

Flooding

The river here is flooding
Water's running high
I've seen this happen once before
Back when I used to cry

I wondered where she moved to
Know I think I know
She's ruined some poor man up the valley
From where these waters flow

El Ninõ- global warming
Sun spots - don't know whether
Been rainin' for a day or two
So it may be the weather

More than likely it's some fool
She's stole another's dream
I feel bad for that lost soul
Whose heart is broke upstream

Fog

This stuff that's falling isn't rain
It's Smoky Mountain fog again
Day to day it can't suspend
And falls to wet the ground and then

It warms to lift into the air
To grow so thick it can't stay there
It fails to float again instead
And falls back down upon my head

And so it goes this mountain mist
Can't make it's mind up just like this
Always here to float around
One day up - the next day down

Ghost Town

The old boards are bleached in the bright devil sun
Their corners are rounded by sand
Tumbleweed bushes are back on the run
And they're racing down Mainstreet again

Doors swing open and old hinges creak
The tin on the roof flops around
A hundred years back it had started to leak
Back before everybody left town

The mines played out, the stagecoach shut down
The railroad passed by to the south
No jobs for the few that straggled around
When they left to put food in their mouth

The rattlesnakes stayed and the lizards are there
They hide in the shade so you never could tell
At night they come out for the cool evening air
When it's quiet as the sand in the well

Then the yellow moon shines in a sky black as ink
And the wind plays tricks in your head
The piano plays soft and the glasses still clink
This ghost town belongs to the dead

Gold

We build our wealth on Wall Street
With stocks both bought and sold
In hopes our worth will multiply
For days when we get old

With careful speculation
In feduciary trust
And some intrepidation
We hope banks don't go bust

Try this reliable trading tip
Invest in friends tenfold
For friends indeed will far exceed
Their mortal worth than gold

Hair

They say our days are numbered
As the hairs upon our head
I lost ten more days today
Just getting out of bed

I'm not looking forward
To death I shall not rush
I saved three thousand days today
When I cleaned out my brush

And on that final day of death
When numbered days are gone
Before I take my final breath
I'll glue it all back on

Hands

These hands have seen some wondrous times
Though aged from scores of years
They worked through grease and grit and grime
Mending life's pistons and gears

They've held the newborn babies
And kept them safe and warm
And rocked them through the dead of night
To ease them through the storms

These hands are scarred from years of trust
Some scars too deep to heal
Bruised as my heart life's hammers crushed
Still trying hard to feel

Honey Bees

Spring is close - it's in the breeze
I'll hack and cough down to my knees
The grass, the trees and flowers, too
I'll cough my head off 'til I'm blue

The great outdoors I love so much
Is pollen's curse to all I touch
I step outside and start to sneeze
Like my nose is full of honey bees

But I'll make do, I'll persevere
I still get through it every year
Just don't laugh when you see me sneeze
And I blow a nose-full of honey bees

I Remember

I remember when Coke was a nickel
And that's all the coke that there was
Shining shoes on Sunday morning
And getting dressed up "just because"

They said if you dream you'll achieve it
But I don't know if that's true
No millionaire here to believe it
Though I hope it can still work for you

I had a whole lifetime to dream it
But that was a lifetime ago
It hasn't turned out like I'd seen it
Still I've come close enough just to know

That love is the cure for what ails you
It's also the cause just as well
And when the dementia avails you
Sweet memories are all shot to hell

Indoor Bath

I took an indoor bath this week
The river is still running cold
The days are warming up enough
I guess I'm just getting old

It rained yesterday and all through the night
It's still too wet to plow
I need a good productive chore
To keep me busy for now

I'd like to spend the day in the loft
There's a banjo and jug of cure
But the old woman's hearing is still too good
She'd give me a tongue lashing sure

It ain't that I don't like to work
It does me good to sweat
But God makes some days into perks
That's why He made rain wet

Maybe I'll start the south field shed
For the two-horse rake and mow
Then when the sides and the roof go up
The jug and the banjo will go

Innocent

I didn't do it - I don't care what they say
It wasn't me - I was elsewhere that day
I am too big around - I'd never have fit
My eyes are the wrong color - I'm innocent, that's it

The footprints show four feet - I only have two
I have a great alibi - hell, I was with you
Whoever was left-handed - I use my right
It was long after dark and I don't drive at night

You say it was carried - that's not gonna bite us
My health hasn't varied - I still have bursitis
My phone didn't ping there and I'll tell you what's worse
I'm innocent dammit - that's just my curse

It's Snowing

It's snowing today in the Great Smoky Mountains
And I fear this time it has stuck
If your fire wood's not cut and stacked up on your porch
My friend, you're just out of luck

The birds are low in the bushes
While the snow is swirling around
The wind in its hurry is blowing the flurries
As they slowly build up on the ground

Warm in my cabin I'm thankful
While outside the cold winds may blow
I have a free day and a banjo to play
And no place calls me to go

It's snowing today in the Great Smoky Mountains
The silence it brings is profound
The trout in the rivers are swimming in shivers
All the evergreen branches bow down

Knowledge

Went to college back in the day
Got some knowledge and threw it away
Found the way to making a choice
Is always listening to my inner voice

Devil on one side - Angel on other
Making a choice is like asking my mother
In money affairs I'm lost in the rough
Too many toys is never enough

Buy it all low and sell it all high
My way to prosper is just getting by
Don't need a fortune, too late for fame
For richer or poorer it's all just the same

Life

If I had it all to do over
I think I probably would
It's not a case if I should
It's not a case if I could

The better parts I'd repeat me
Improve on the places I failed
Do combat with things to defeat me
And cherish the parts that I nailed

The problem is I enjoyed it
The love and the passions perfumed
But I didn't study my history
Thank goodness I'm bound to be doomed

Lizard

Pine lizard scrambles up the tree
Peeks around to look at me
I move around and try to hide
And grab him from the other side

Lizard's chest is green and blue
He's scared and doesn't know what to do
I let him bite and I yell real loud
Got to make the lizard proud

Place him back upon the pine
He's almost like a friend of mine
He's got lots of tales to tell
He made the monster giant yell

Love Is

Love is power, love is action
Love is hope's unfettered traction
Love is clouds and wings to soar
Until love isn't anymore

Then love is smoke and love is mirrors
Love is sheep before the shearers
Love is shine without the buffing
Love is all or love is nothing

Give love free to those who sought
To buy a heart that won't be bought
.And don't cash in your mortal checks
From yard sale finds no heart respects

But give it all as chance permits
And dream of round holes square plugs fit
No one can tell when love is true
Except for one - that one is you

Love's Illusions

Love's illusion - oh, there's a thrill
Pretend you had love as you will
Moan and wail to show your grief
Search for another to find relief

Ride that new wave to the shore
Over your head and still want more
Shoot the pipe and hanging ten
And wipe out deep - you've lost again

You bought her map - X marks the spot
And fell in the trap so you dig a lot
Hopes are high as love expects
The closer you get - she moves the X

So pluck the last petal - she loves me not
I don't have to settle for what I've got
It's not my fault love isn't fair
I cannot have lost what wasn't there

New Age

Astral charts and zodiac signs
Reading tea leaves and hand palm lines
Colored auras and psychic glow
Rubies, moonstone and peridot

Meditation, hugging trees
A greater love so hard to please
Mother Nature's grand commune
Someday tides will pull the moon

Lotus powder, namaste
Incense chase bad luck away
Who is it that thinks this stuff?
New Age living must be rough

New Old Year

All that's old the thirty-first
Bids farewell and breaks the curse
To greet the New Year strong and bold
And end the old year's icy hold

The cares and worries fade to black
In hopes they never do come back
And freshly starts a cleaner slate
Where hope eternal points our fate

And yet our habits still unbroken
Break all promises unspoken
Last year's path we march again
Our pasts and futures hand in hand

Nightfall

Dark and tragic misty magic
Nightfall fades within my hollow
Dawning starts in sleepy hearts
As sunlight marks the day to follow

Signs of hope to help me cope
A new day dawns upon my lap
Through time and space and God's own Grace
From Clingmans Dome to Newfound Gap

And though winds blow trees to and fro
To float the hawks plumb out of sight
The light will end - hawks will descend
When darkness brings another night

Noel

The kids are home for Christmas
With spirits bright as neon
Someone rearranged the candles
So now they spell out LEON

They're full of tricks an' cheerfulness
I know there'll be more pranks
I'll offer up the dinner prayer
So God will get the thanks

And sometime Christmas morning
When the wrapping papers fly
I'll remind them of the Reason
Or at least I know I'll try

Soon after kids will pack and go
Continuing on their quest
The decorations all come down
And LEON gets a rest

Normal

Normal is as normal does
It wasn't then until it was
Sociologists read the trends
Then change their minds and make amends

What's wrong is right, what's right is wrong
So you've been normal all along
Whoever you are just stay that way
Some point in time you'll be OK

Nothing

Today I did twice as much nothing
As the nothing I did 'day before
Tomorrow I'll do three times the nothing
Or maybe just possibly more

It does take a whole lot of planning
But I can do that in my head
If I do it just right I'll finish tonight
With nothing keeping me from bed

When I look back on my accomplishment
I revel in a great job well done
Not all can succeed in doing nothing they need
Even when doing nothing is fun

All my life I've done nothing
With nothing my ultimate goal
Nearing seventy fast, my youth may soon pass
And I'll enjoy doing nothing when I'm old

Panning

I've panned for gold in Georgia
In Dahlonega for dust
And north in Carolina
Where the panning was a bust

And still the tales of wonder
Where the gems and gold flow free
Keeps my gold pan dipping under
For a glint of gold for me

It's addictive like the lotto
Where the odds are naught to none
But I've made it my own motto
Keep on panning while it's fun

Paper

I don't read the paper
All the news is sad
The comics aren't funny
And the sports is just as bad

Politics is dirty
Religion's getting mean
Wall Street wants to screw us all
And government is a scheme

American business fires us
They have to save their cheese
The companies that do hire us
Have their office overseas

They say the Earth is warming
But they don't pay my heat
They screw my gas with ethanol
And pump water in my meat

They GMO my veggies
And kill the honey bees
I'll read the friggin' paper
When they stop cutting down my trees

Pencil Strike

I stare it down, it just stares back
I don't think it gives a damn
What once enlightened now turned black
Is locked up tighter than a clam

It once wrote script in fluid line
With deepened thought and lyric fair
Yet now it is not so inclined
This pencil has no words to share

It acts as if it's gone on strike
Perhaps it means to pay me back
For stupid words I didn't like
Erasing lines, removing black

The joke's on you my graphite friend
No writings flounder on your rocks
No weary words on you depend
There's nine fresh pencils in your box

People

We're people of color whoever we are
We offend one another up close and afar
It doesn't come natural - we practice the skill
'Til it's honed to an art - until one word can kill

We get along well until someone's lost face
And we don't have an answer and then we yell "race"
Conversation diverted - the problem's still there
So it's never resolved and just hangs in the air

And that's how it is and always shall be
There are those among us who cannot be free
When challenged we rush to imprison our lot
It's a comfortable warm blanket - it's all that we've got

PhD

I got a PhD in hindsight
From the school of Don't Look Back
Taught me all I soon forgot
About stayin' on the track

The present 's not so pleasant
My future yet arrives
I can't move fast to leave the past
It's where I'm still alive

When you cannot focus forward
Where everything looks strange
It's plenty thrill to just stand still
And never suffer change

You can't see where you're going
If you don't know where you been
'Til I can see what I want to be
I'll keep looking back again

Red Tail

In the heat of the day as the fog burns away
The birds stop their song for a time
When they hear the hawk shreak and in fear of his beak
They watch as he circles and climbs

Off into the sky he floats up so high
The rabbits and squirrels think he's gone
They resume before us their song and their chorus
And life in the mountains goes on

Then without a sound a streak hits the ground
The red tails wings begin flappin'
As he carries aloft his dinner so soft
Mister rabbit never knew what just happened

Reindeer

All year long I celebrate
With cooking up a stew
Rabbit, squirrel, quail and dove
With luck a hog or two

The winter though, my favorite time
I cook a special treat
For Christmas is one time each year
That brings me reindeer meat

Last year was a good one
I got lucky I suppose
I shot the leading reindeer
With the bright and shiny nose

He turned out kinda skinny
Not much meat upon the bone
But by the time I loaded
The whole damned herd had flown

The fat red hunter in the red sled
Was yelling for them to slow
'Cause as he chased them through the night
He was hollerin' "Ho......HO......HOOOOOOOO......."

REM

REM sleep - What I need
A deeper rest the whole night through
Joke's on me if I succeed
And only have more dreams of you

Tossed and rolling in the sheets
Wheels are turning as I linger
The little hand points: 3 AM
The big hand giving me the finger

Serves me right to love you after
Serves me right for loves replay
Daylight comes and still I bring her
In cherished memories of the day

Restaurant Rules

Restaurants have too many rules
There's problems there I say
Like "No Solicitation"
Then they solicit me to pay

No shoes, no shirt, no service
The sign on each door rants
But I still get my coffee
If I just forgot my pants

And now they say "No Smoking"
What genius thought that up?
There goes my special booth
Where I could smoke and drink a cup

The waiters all want their tips
So how can this be fair?
It's just a cup of coffee dude
You walked from here to there

Yep, nowadays I stay at home
My rules are more than token
No pay, no pants, no tips at all
And I drink my coffee smokin'

Rewind

I love living life backwards
It's funner to live in reverse
Where you do all the early stuff later
And start with the later things first

I wake up early for coffee
Then straight back to bed for more sleep
At noon I cook myself breakfast
This plan isn't really that deep

I lived all my later years early
Grew up like a grandpa on rules
Now I'm catching my teen years up surely
Can't get kicked out of retirement school

I eat my dessert and then dinner
And I mix in my coffee with wine
Of course I'm not getting much thinner
But it makes growing younger feel fine

Rhododendron

Rhododendron, mountain laurel
Roots dig in where none else will
Therein stone-bound lies the moral
Here up high on Heaven's sill

Progress comes, progress goes
God's creation suffers all
We hug the rock where our faith grows
In aged stone the angels call

First to see the sun at rise
Last to see it's full retreat
Blessed by Smoky Mountain skies
Comfort from our Mercy Seat

Schedule

It's 9AM in the morning
Looks like I slept late again
I need to be cooking my breakfast
But I'll put it off long as I can

There's important things to be doing
Like watching the river roll by
Or smelling my coffee that's brewing
Watching fog float up to the sky

I hate to be thought of as lazy
This talent took years to aquire
Until I start pushing up daisies
My job is to teach and inspire

I'd set up a channel on YouTube
But I'm nekkid right down to my toes
Alone in these rooms in my Fruit Of the Looms
It takes too much time to wear clothes

So I reach to my students in poem
With a talent surreal and prehensile
'Til someday they say "Yeh, I know him
And he writes with a pretty sharp pencil"

Silent Eve

Kaleidoscoping crystals fall
From midnight velvet blackened sky
To cover sleepy mountains all
With winter's screaming silenced cry

The crunch of snow beneath the boot
Then firewood tumbles to the floor
The crackling fireplace smoking mute
Will dance with spark and flame once more

The book aside and covers beckon
Warmth and sleep a good day's end
Til sunlight comes with sounds to reckon
And one more mountain day begins

Tempus Fugit

Tempus fugit so they say
Until they find a better way
Who has the time for verbal satin
For those of us who don't speak Latin

Time will come and always passes
Gapping most of life's crevasses
Slowing last as cold molasses
Following Holy DNA patent

And vaguely watching apoplexic
My kitchen calendar dyslexic
Thursdays turn to Monday morn
Still lusting eggs and sausage porn

'Til rudely comes the knock on door
I go to answer yet once more
And halt with calm that last decision
It's someone on the television

Time moves on - this is tomorrow
So many from my calendar borrowed
Another trick of timeless sages
Stolen future calendar pages

The Dream

I had a dream of her last night
The dream was so disjointed
But everything turned out all right
I wasn't disappointed

I woke up feeling almost sick
And didn't understand
Until it hit me like a brick
I had that dream again

It's painful how the wrong I've done
Follows as age climbs
A teenage boy just thinks of fun
But I've paid ten thousand times

Her rods were knocking – she needed work
How low can one man stoop?
Instead of saving - this teenage jerk
Sold his 1940 Ford Coupe

The Path

The stones we stumbled on in youth
Keep showing up with age and worse
The path we walk in search of truth
We sometimes travel in reverse

With twisted ankles, bruised toes
We watch old dreams become unraveled
Knowing now in brief repose
There's reasons that this path's less travelled

We've bought the spiel the sages speak
To claw and climb that trail until
We learn their joke upon life's peak
The path to home is all down hill

The Thief

Cherry pie - I best not risk it
Safer here to steal a biscuit
Buttered up and jellied down
Eat it quiet - don't make a sound

Big ole plate once held a dozen
Now I'm hungry for its cousin
Stack 'em high they count to ten
Better not do this again

Once again the thief is caught
I snuck my best or so I thought
When asked what fact precedes my doom
She points "The crumbs lead to your room"

Valentine

My dearest darling Valentine
I'm writing you this poem
Of love for you and heartfelt thanks
The facts just as I know 'em

I try my best this time each year
To tell of my affection
By giving you some chocolates
A sweet and grand confection

But like years past I bought too soon
This gift of love so sweetened
That by this so important day
Your chocolates are all eaten

Valley

I live in a high mountain valley
The streets are all paved with gold
The flowers in the shade are orange marmalade
So our biscuits never get cold

The sidewalks are made out of sugar
There's coffee on everyone's porch
And tho' it sounds risky the lampposts flow whiskey
At night we light them with a torch

Everyone's wealthy in my town
The money grows on the trees
Spring and summer are fine but the fall is divine
When the money piles up to our knees

We held an election for mayor
Everyone ran and they won
The first law we wrote was to outlaw the vote
Then retired as our work was all done

If you're ever nearby stop and visit
There's always plenty to do
There's plenty to see and the restaurants are all free
All our mirrors are reflections of you

Writer's Block

A thousand pages brilliant white
Laughing at me in the night
Taunting, pointing at the clock
Feeling safe for writer's block

I wait until they fall asleep
And grab two sheets for me to keep
Imagine of their gasping horror
To find I've written come tomorrow

With nothing here that's worth the write
I'll jot that down and just for spite
To use poor grammar, misspelled words
And metaphors that no one's heard

If just to mess up paper more
Unleash the hogs of verbal war
To rape the night in moments spent
In search of forked compliment

ABOUT THE AUTHOR

I started my appreciation of poetry in high school when I read works of Longfellow, Byron, Poe and Lovelace and the like. I was writing songs for my music group of high school friends, we played at restaurants and parties and won the WSB radio "Hootenanny" competition two years in a row at the Southeastern fair in Atlanta.

In 1965 I moved to Nashville to further my education and got in with more guitar pickers from around the "Music City." A publisher heard one of my songs at a party and then it was recorded one week later and I was hired to work for the record label. Over two years I submitted only twelve songs, but eleven of them were recorded, in many cases by several artists.

At one time I had three songs in the top 100 Billboard magazine and the Top 60 country list in Record World magazine at the same time. They were "Wax Museum," "And Say Goodbye" and "My Baby." Most writers back then struggled to get one song in the charts in a lifetime, and here I had three at one time. I was walking in tall cotton.

I was blessed to meet many big name stars. I met with and picked most evenings with Chris Gantry when we would write separately at his large house or we'd end up at someone else's place to jam. We picked many times at Kris Kristofferson's apartment. Soon after that was when Kristofferson wrote his "Sunday Morning Coming Down" and almost everything he touched turned to gold after that.

I picked a little bit at work with Eddie Rabbit before he hit it big and I knew Vern Gosdin and Bill Carlisle. The New York label that bought out Chart Records sent two ladies to Nashville to record a country album and they both recorded my songs. The ladies were Jeanie Ewing and Cyd Charisse.

I had lost two girlfriends to drugs from the music business, so when I met the girl I wanted to marry there was only one way to protect her and that meant leaving the music industry. So I did. I should have stayed in the business.

Grant King works and lives in Jackson County, North Carolina, in the Great Smoky Mountains.

www.ingramcontent.com/pod-product-compliance
Lightning Source LLC
Chambersburg PA
CBHW032020090426
42741CB00006B/678